THE SNOWBOUND HOUSE

To Pat --
What a pleasure to
see you again! Thank you
so much for coming tonight

Shara

May 2012

ANHINGA PRESS

THE SNOWBOUND HOUSE

SHANE SEELY

2008 Philip Levine for Poetry

Selected by
Dorianne Laux

ANHINGA PRESS
TALLAHASSEE, FLORIDA 2009

Cover art: *Northern Lights,* 18" X 24" acrylic on canvas by Heather Ross
Author photograph: Corinne Wohlford Taff
Cover design and production: C.L. Knight
Text design and typesetting: Jill Runyan
Type Styles: titles and text set In Adobe Caslon Pro

Library of Congress Cataloging-in-Publication Data
The Snowbound House by Shane Seely – First Edition
ISBN – 978-1-934695-14-2
Library of Congress Cataloging Card Number – 2009935036

This publication is sponsored in part by a grant
from the Florida Department of State,
Division of Cultural Affairs, and the Florida Arts Council.

Anhinga Press Inc. is a nonprofit corporation dedicated wholly to the pub-
lication and appreciation of fine poetry and other literary genres.

For personal orders, catalogs
and information write to:
Anhinga Press
P.O. Box 10595
Tallahassee, Florida 32302
Web site: www.anhinga.org
E-mail: info@anhinga.org

Published in the United States
by Anhinga Press
Tallahassee, Florida
First Edition, 2009

for my parents
and in memory of theirs

THE PHILIP LEVINE PRIZE FOR POETRY

The annual competition for the Philip Levine Prize for Poetry is sponsored and administered by the M.F.A. Program in Creative Writing at California State University, Fresno.

2008
Shane Seely
The Snowbound House
Selected by Dorianne Laux

2007
Neil Aitken
The Lost Country of Sight
Selected by C.G. Hanzlicek

2006
Lynn Aarti Chandhok
The View from Zero Bridge
Selected by Corrinne Clegg Hales

2005
Roxane Beth Johnson
Jubilee
Selected by Philip Levine

2002
Steven Gehrke
The Pyramids of Malpighi
Selected by Philip Levine

2001
Fleda Brown
Breathing In, Breathing Out
Selected by Philip Levine

Contents

Three

Acknowledgments

The author thanks the following publications, in which some
of these poems first appeared or are forthcoming, sometimes in
different versions:

5 AM: "The Valley"
Arts & Letters: "On Reading Jeffers' 'The Excesses of God,'"
    "The Celebration"
Bellingham Review: "Six Mornings"
Blue Earth Review: "The Driver from the Rendering Plant"
Center: A Journal of the Literary Arts: "The Darkness of the Room"
Chautauqua Literary Journal: "The Rooster," "The Last Meal
    of François Mitterand," "A Theater of Ghosts"
Clackamas Literary Review: "West Nile"
Dislocate: "Leavings"
Flint Hills Review: "In Shadow"
Image: "Second Attempt at Elegy for Anthony Piccione,"
    "We Shall Not All Sleep"
Marlboro Review: "Dirt," "Photo: Deer Season, Age 13"
Notre Dame Review: "First Attempt at Elegy for Anthony Piccione"
    (as "Elegy for Anthony Piccione")
Passages North: "Against Reading"
Poems & Plays: "The Clawfoot Tub"
Prairie Schooner: "The Beech Nut"
River Styx: "Two Boys in the Woods"
Roger: "What Memory, What Mark"
Salamander: "Flint Hills"
The Seattle Review: "Above Ground"
Southern Poetry Review: "Dowsing"
Sou'wester: "Dairy Farm, January"
Water~Stone: "Written On the Eve of the Cassini Space Launch"
West Branch: "Hollow Bones," "Elegy and Spade"
Willow Springs: "For a Burial"

"The Last Meal of François Mitterand" also was featured on the
Poetry Daily web site (www.poems.com).

I would like to thank Dorianne Laux, Corrinne Clegg Hales, and the creative writing program at Fresno State for their generous readings of the manuscript. Thanks to Rick Campbell, Lynne Knight, and everyone else at Anhinga Press for their patience, intelligence, and expertise. My gratitude to Heather Ross for her beautiful art and for her enthusiasm about the book. Thanks also to Elizabeth Dodd; to my comrades at Syracuse; to Brooks Haxton, Mary Karr, Michael Burkard, George Saunders and Malena Mörling; to my Saint Louis readers, past and present: Chuck Sweetman, Joel Friederich, Corinne Taff, Jason Sommer, Lisa Ampleman, Lisa Pepper, Terry Quinn, and Jeff Hamilton; to my wonderful WashU colleagues; and to Sonia, for every page.

I had a terror — since September — I could tell no one —
and so I sing, as the Boy does by the Burying Ground.
— *Emily Dickinson*

ONE

FIRST ATTEMPT AT ELEGY FOR ANTHONY PICCIONE

Out by the lake, the graves of soldiers
lurch in thaw.

Their bodies
are uneasy with the weather,

and their souls —
I cannot tell you where their souls have gone.

If the grass
shaded by this gravestone

is a song,
then who will hear it?

I do not speak
that tongue.

We suspect the dead are singing.
A high pine

sways inside the wind.
There are hollow sounds in the eaves.

If there is singing
after death, and souls gone somewhere

past the great thatch of cloud
above the lake

can pitch a tune,
why sorrow for the dead

and all their poems?
Their poems live, even

when their song is wind —
but here, we spade fresh dirt

onto a grave
and tunnel deeper into our lives.

I suspect the dead don't sing
and can only hold their heads

in disbelief
at what they have become.

For _____,
Who Fell From a Bridge above the Mississippi

I wonder
    what attitude
        you adopted as you fell,

and if you prayed
    to be turned
        into a bird or into liquid

and, if you prayed,
    to whom.
        Did you, as the wind

ripped harder at your skin,
    imagine God's cupped hands
        coalescing

in the air above the water?
    Did you see the sky
        reflected in the river's face

and forget
    a moment
        that you were not flying?

Or, as the sunlight
    fractured on the river
        rising toward you,

did you howl
    like the animal
        you were?

As you broke
        the pane of water
                and were untethered

from yourself,
        did your mouth
                taste of vinegar?

Did you seek
        a threshold
                and find dark water?

THE SNOWBOUND HOUSE

Inside the wall, a mouse
pulls its tail across its eyes. Its heartbeat

has grown so slow, the thump
so far from the reciprocal

thump, that it might be two mice asleep
in separate walls, in separate nests

of chewed insulation, hoarding separate
caches of grain. All summer,

the goldenrod, the larkspur, the yellow rattle
grew tall in fields left fallow. Bees

lingered in the mouths
of the horse nettle in the yard.

Beneath the porch, a fox
killed a family of rabbits, left only

tufts of hair, a few scattered ribs.
When winter came,

snow piled at the edges of the porch,
gathered in drifts

to the windows, to the eaves.
He returns

to find the front door buried
beneath snow drifted hard. The barn

leans in the wind. As he climbs
the drift, he remembers the tableau:

his father hunched in coveralls, carving
a path from house to barn. Through

a second-story window, he enters
an empty room. His breath

frosts patterns on the glass, obscuring
the barn, the car, his track across the snow.

It is as cold inside
as out.

AFTER READING JEFFERS' "THE EXCESSES OF GOD"

1

The oil leaking
from the Evinrude
spreads a rainbow
on the water. Such
is the divine excess
of God, the shimmering
colors dissipating back
into His mind
as I churn across
the lake. It is cold,
spring in the North,
the air redolent
of casket mud and moss
on new stones
in the early thaws.
The water's turning
over. I cast, and the spoon
turns, casts back the light
brilliantly, an unnecessary
gesture, before it drops
into the water
and I retrieve it.

2

To the pike's savage athletics
in the bottom of my boat
I respond with gaff
and pliers, reach to drop him
back into his darkness.
His scales are immaculate,

a delicate mosaic of white
and the muddy green of
water grass:
no signature, no smudge
of the painter's thumb,
a fact which might be testament
to the artist's skill. I release him
and he dives. Along the jaw
of the pliers, mouth-blood glistens:
for God so loved the world
that even blood
must be as bright as flowers.

Two Boys in the Woods

find a rifle shell darkly gleaming in the leaves.
Breathy, they pocket it as though it were a curl
of a lover's hair.
For days they take turns keeping it,
sleeping with it standing upright on the nightstand
or tucked beneath a pillow,
holding it to the light
to study the brassy casing, the sleek nose of the bullet.
Each boy dreams
of the bullet's shrieking arc,
how it tears at the air
as it flies. They carry it
to school, eat their meals with it cradled
in a palm.
Finally, in the darkness of a roadside field,
one boy tapes a three-penny nail to the butt end of the shell,
point against the primer, and grips the casing
with his father's pliers.
The other boy wields a ball-peen hammer.
The strike is clean.
When the shell explodes,
the pliers split at the hinge, and the hammer's poll shatters.
One boy's hand opens into the darkness,
gloved in blood,
while the boy with the broken hammer
discovers he's alive.

Six Mornings

1

The bright carp raise a fin out of the water
and turn their creamy gray-white mouths
toward the newly gilded clouds
assembling in the sky above the garden.
They are hungry, as they are always hungry,
sucking at the air which must taste
like the rind of the world. A Red-winged Blackbird
sways from a cattail, singing
of its shining scar.
Morning distills in a rivulet of dew
along the shallow cleft of a water lily's leaf,
shivers in the sun, and runs without a sound
into the forgetful pond.

2
We wake up fighting

last night's fight.
We're up quickly, naked (having

slept so, even at such
odds — the body
craving closeness all the more), stalking
room to room, slamming doors, cold

breakfast at the sink, shouting
through the shower curtain, through a mouth
of toothpaste —

outside, the sun bruises the trees.

3

Downtown, the blank faces of the buildings
catch fire in the sunrise: they blush
to be revealed so — naked, stupid, greedy, rude —
each morning.
They raise themselves to their full height
as if to make the best
of an uncomfortable situation,

and the sun admires them a little
for their ugly confidence.
The buildings fill their bellies
with people, which flutter and hum like bees
worrying their sticky combs.

4

sun through east window   sheet

                              languid across your body

tips of subtle fingers

                       the length of morning

fruit peeled in bed and eaten

                              sleep and then

more sleep   morning

                       as indulgence

5

Another spade of dirt

                       on the hummocks of the dead,
the root pulled from the ditch at the building's edge

                                        still tree-bound,
craning toward sunlight: what

                       are the dead

                              to me?

At the height of their power, the ancient Egyptians
                          believed each evening the sun burnt up.
What miracle each morning, then: the sun
                          rekindled, a fresh torch for the day.

        We bury
the dead with each waking —

                          tread the ground,

let the sun burn on.
From dirt we rise each day

    6
and so we fall.

What burns in us
burns.
        Today my grandfather

wakes dizzy with morphine, his face describing his skull, his tongue
dry against his worn teeth. He wakes
                          worn, unsure
        of waking, shrouded figures haunting the light
from the window, which he still knows faces west.
Were he lucid, he would be
                          annoyed with God,
        with his preparations for his death,
                          with the seemingly interminable
wait. His legs are slender
like the legs of young cattle, and his head
                          is heavy.

His eyes, small blue coins,
        flutter and then close.

        And then the rising
into morning.

HOLLOW BONES

In the weed beds, carp lean
into the air, come plashing
back against the glassy water.
Two gar drift delicate as flutes
in shallows warmed all day by sun. From
across the bay a heron
wings its hollow bones toward shore
and sets down croaking for the night.
I am heartened
by the indifference of this place to me,
as though I were the swarm of gnats
above the bed of lily pads, spinning the air to wool.
All day the sun has burned my neck
with no particular desire, and now the moon
rises with its bucket full,
just as it would if I were dead, or president, or
somewhere else. A Red-winged Blackbird
flutters from the rushes,
picks an insect from the air.
I am no more than I am.

DESERT ALMANAC
—for Nate

When the earth   throws a shadow on the moon
            while at the same time a comet   burns across one corner
of the twilit sky

and coyotes as the star parade begins   open their throats
            across the mesa   it is good to be beside a fire
with a friend who knows how to be quiet

it is good to let the desert night   blossom above you

to watch sparks from the fire   address the stars as their beloveds
            and as the comet brightens   as the sky grows darker

and the earth's shadow   begins to slide from the moon's face
            it is good to be   as quiet as you can
not to move or speak or think

and to let the coyotes   do your singing for you

WRITTEN ON THE EVE
OF THE CASSINI SPACE LAUNCH

*In February 1997, NASA launched the Cassini Space Probe,
laden with 64 pounds of plutonium fuel and headed on a
seven-year journey to Saturn.*

Perhaps it will be gone by morning,
perhaps in seven years we will have crawled
into the lap of the old god, the grandfather,
and peeked beneath his fingernails: dirty ice,
methane, old chunks of moon, something dead,
something about to be.
                              When I was seven,
I saw it through a telescope, the pale yellow
hint of a form. My father swore
it could not be true.
                              Or perhaps the morning will cough,
and the trails of white smoke will disappoint,
like bottle rockets in the afternoon, and the edge of each sky
will flush just a little, and children will watch, not expecting
to be devoured.
                              My father thought it was a fake,
a yellow cutout on the big lens. But when a man stepped in front,
the whole thing disappeared.

A Theater of Ghosts

As I walked outside to see the dogs to bed,
there, in the cleft of the valley, glowed
the northern lights, green
as green glass washed in a dark sea.
The dogs nosed around the larch tree
where a squirrel had rested in the afternoon.
I wondered what the natives of this place
had seen on nights like this — new moon, brittle
cold, sheets of color shifting in the sky:
a fire in the gods' house? a theater
of ghosts? What meaning had they made
of the colors billowing and swirling
above pines plunged in a blackness
I will never know? Those colors seemed as strange
as speech or music, and I wanted them
to sing to me. So I waited in the cold
until my knuckles stiffened, my white breath
dissipating at my lips. The sky flickered
green to yellow, on to blue: mute, distant
and expansive. In the field beyond
the stream, a fox barked, and I want
to say it sounded lonely. Deer
browsed beneath the gnarled apples
just beyond the yard. I was the only animal
looking up.

Flint Hills

Fire is grazing tonight
along the prairie ridge.

Shepherds bearing shovels
herd it toward the fencerow,

then away. From this distance,
it seems a long fuse burning

from one end of the dark field
to the other, as if once

it has burned, something
will explode. There is no quiet

like the quiet of these plains.
To the south,

on the fenced-in Konza,
a small herd of bison

beds down
among the bluestem,

and the cottonwoods
are silent

along the Kansas and the Blue.
This is the land

that broke the settlers'
plows, and whatever sod

was lifted was returned
above a grave.

I am too distant
to hear them talk along the fire line,

and the darkness is too deep
for them to see me.

There are only the sounds of tires
howling on I-70,

as far off
and as constant as the dead.

The Valley

What seeped into the valley that night touched everything
    within it. It touched the stream, and the old tire
in the stream, and the bubbles that the water made
    as it flowed around the tire.
It was not smoke, or fog, or a chemical
    gas, but it rose through the valley
to touch the stone foundations of the barns,
    their plank walls, and sheet-metal roofs
painted silver. The rabbits sleeping in the tall grasses
    were touched without their knowing, as were
the tall grasses, and the dew that dusk had left
    on them. All the trees alike were touched: oaks and hemlocks,
maples with their sweetly flowing sap,
    elms and beech, ironwoods and apples.
It touched the tender skin beneath the elbow of a flying squirrel
    that scavenged seeds among the pines, eyes wide in the moonlight,
and it touched the light of the moon and stars.
    It moved down the road, covering the asphalt laid by men
who had leaned in shade against their shovels, entering
    all of its crevices. It touched the people in their houses as they slept
or watched TV, and their pianos, silent now, some out of tune,
    and the swallows nesting in the eaves. It crossed
the Amish family's uncut fields and filled their house
    and barn, and touched the coarsely whiskered muzzles
of the Belgians leaning in their clapboard stalls.
    All it touched was turned to sorrow: sad
water, sad barns, sad rabbits in the tall, sad grass.
    It filled the valley until it found one man,
my uncle, sleeping in his father's house, and pooled
    inside his ears, filled his mouth and nose, touched
the tiny filaments inside his lungs. And as he slept,
    his dreams began to change.

Two

THE LESSON

I was young when my father called me to the back door
to show me the brain of the white-tailed deer

he had shot and had been flaying
in the garage. He had hacksawed off

the skull's cap to save the antlers, which he would nail,
once the little flap of hide had peeled away,

beside the others on the wall. The brain
was smallish, wrinkled, gelatin; it oozed

into the board he'd laid it on. He touched it lightly
with his hunting knife, and caused a little slit

to open around the knife's tip. I wondered
if anything remained: the detailed sketches

of each rise and crevice of the hills; the language
of scent and gesture; the image of my father

as he raised his gun and fired. We stood
in silence, the mute brain congealing between us,

my father holding it toward me as if to say,
Look, son, this is the world.

WHAT MEMORY, WHAT MARK

The rabbit sits wild-eyed in the multiflora rose
because we hunt it, my cousin and I,
wearing blue jeans and carrying
.22 rifles. This old pasture is sectioned
by low stone walls, stacks of mossy sandstone tablets
prized from the ground years ago
by the strong men who settled here,
who raised the first barns and built homes
for their sad young wives, who fathered sons
and cursed the cold and shoveled shit
into ditches, who damned
playing cards and dancing as the devil's
pleasures. My cousin pokes a stick
into the rose bush, while I stand
with rifle shouldered, squinting
at the bead. Later, strong men in trucks
will come and haul away the stone
to landscape poolside patios
in the bedroom communities of New Jersey.
I spare no thought for the walls,
but to spend a moment steadying
a shot on one. Only
after they've been harvested
will I think of the rough hands of the haulers
bundling the stone, loading it on pallets
for the truck, and of my ancestors
walking the fencerows after a thaw,
lifting rocks with their own rough hands
to build the wall again, filling gaps
with small or odd-shaped stones

to bring the line to true. I will think of the soft feet
of the families walking toward their pools
in the soft light of a suburban morning,
and wonder what stone carries bundled with it
as it's trucked away — what memory, what mark
of having been taken from this ground,
held with those hands, stacked
into that moss-furred wall. My cousin stabs
the multiflora with his stick. The rabbit
flushes. I squeeze the trigger slowly.
When the rabbit stops running, I fire.

DEER SPOTTING

Nights in summer, we crept in cars and pickup trucks
down dirt back roads, cones of light blazing
from our windows to the woods-edge
that a narrow field of corn or pasture ran against.
We didn't carry guns, just spots, and binoculars, perhaps,
and a driving urge to drive a hole into the dark to see
into the lives of white-tailed deer: a buck in velvet
feeding in the stubble of a hayed field, a doe and her fawn
leaping a wire fence to disappear behind a curtain of maples.
We were reverently quiet, only counting to ourselves
their shadows if we talked at all. The deer
raised their faces from their browse to watch us,
their eyes glowing green in the spotlight. Come fall, the men
would slip into the woods at dawn and drag their bodies out
to happy families, photos in the weekly paper.
But on these nights,
we only watched them, moved by their calm,
by their delicate faces, by the ghostly grace
with which they moved from our world
into the dark corridors of theirs.

THE BEECH NUT

I did not imagine
such hands could be so delicate

as he cracked the beech nut open
and offered me the tiny jewel of meat inside.

His palm was a field
left fallow through the winter,

in which I might watch white-tailed deer
leap a fence or linger into dusk.

With a finger the girth and color
of a shovel handle, he nudged

the burred husk
and pried the soft nut free.

Those hands, which I had seen
wring a chicken's neck

as though they were returning the cap
to the jug of milk in the refrigerator.

Those hands, which I had seen
fix tractors, fell hemlocks,

lead cattle to their slaughter
by the horn.

The beech nut tasted
exactly as the forest smelled

that sun-ripe day
early in the winter: earthy, a little sweet,

with an overtone of something just beyond
my apprehension.

Years later he would wait
with my mother and the hospice nurse

for death to come. With his hands
he would smooth the care-home's gown,

the color of a sky
in which the clouds are stained with blue

by the indefatigable sun, or he would fold
his hands across his chest.

Other times he would raise those hands
before his eyes

and say to the shadows in the room,
What can a strong man do to leave this life?

ELEGY AND SPADE

A grave is dug one morning deep.
The ground is gouged,
and they lower the old man
down. The dirt,

the sweet-smelling loam of his country,
is replaced above him.
These become the layers
of his atmosphere:

the pleated ceiling of the casket,
the thick lacquer of the wood,
the airy soil and eventual grass,
the living hovering above the grave

which might be the gap in the earth
that the casket holds,
or the mound in shade above,
or something else —

then trees which will die in their own bark
rising, trailing shadows,
and a column of sky so tall it looks blue
with one sailing sorrowful cloud.

The minister, head low, hands pious,
says they didn't lower him down,
but returned what he had borrowed once he'd left.
I saw him, though, his body

rouged and pillowed:
the crooked nose, the huge, delicate hands,
the one finger ruined by the harrow.
He descended

and the earth was returned to him.
He was lowered
and a shovel
scraped his name.

A man
makes a grave —

the earth
he is.

In Shadow

The moon, two nights from full, is tangled in the dark
arms of the pin oak. Through the sooted
membrane of my window, it refracts:
around the glowing ovoid, a scattering of after-
images, as though someone had smudged it
with a thumb. I am thinking tonight
of that barest darkened crescent,
that slivered paring, absent, still
singing to the sea —

and of my grandfather,
lightened by the weight
of his soul, the man and the not-man,
the merest husk, laid out on the table
at the Fickinger Funeral Home,
his hair combed, his skin ash,
and of the room of people
trying to reconcile his presence with his absence.

THE EMBRACE

He's long gone:
the body laid beneath
a taciturn Protestant
headstone, the farm sold
at the first offer.
The same sort
of headstone marks
my father's plot
in the same cemetery,
one number left
unchiseled. My father
never wanted to be
his father. None
of us does. One man
might take a country to war
to not become his father,
while another might only
leave the farm for college
and not return.
Another man might pay
a man to change the oil
in his car: it doesn't matter.
What matters is that one day
when I, a grown man,
was standing at my car, ready
to retreat across the broad
and broadening gap
between my life and his,
my father reached past
the hand I offered him
and — shyly, almost —
put his arms

around my ribs
and, saying nothing,
held me there.
Only later did I learn
of the dream he'd had
the night before,
in which his father returned.
In the dream, my father tried
to put his arms
around his father, to feel
the strange sensation
of his cheek
against his father's cheek.
But some force held them
apart, as with two magnets
of the same polarity.
And so that morning my father
drew himself toward me
and held us there. Each of us
closed his eyes, as though in dream.

DIRT

In my memory's memory, it is always
dark. The walls are unpainted,
the furniture bare. By the light of a sooty
lamp, my ancestors pray before their hard
beds, their knuckles barked
and scabbed, their hands bent
from their tools. Outside, a cow lowers
her head to brittle grass, and the disced field
begins to dry. My wife says, *My*
grandfather browned his hands in that
dirt, that dirt your people owned.
And they came, her people, dirt-dark
and full of sorrow (I imagine I remember), pulling
back the earth until the life emerged, hard
and knobby in their hard and knobby hands.
But my people less owned the dirt
than the dirt owned them, pulled
at the cuffs of their coveralls always
down, always burden, always load. Dirt
shoveled. Dirt piled and hauled.
Dirt spaded over. My wife's grandfather
turned the dirt my fathers owned,
the dirt they died in. *Come back, come back,*
the dirt sang, and each returned.

Photo: Deer Season, Age 13

This is the photo of me
next to the doe I killed
with my father's rifle.
My father aimed the camera,
took his prize: that's his
shadow on the snow.
The gun is laid aside,
outside the frame,
quiet, sulfurous, waiting
to be cleaned. In the center
of the image is a ghost, a trace:
not the missing
gun, nor the father
who frames the scene,
through whose squinting eye
we view boy and deer.
The doe's protruding tongue
says *form*, says *carcass*:
empty shell. She left
through a keyhole
between her ribs. She is not
the center of the picture.
I am the ghost the image haunts,
who tore loose from the photoed body
and went beyond, beyond —
look how they reflect
the slanting winter sun:
the doe's dead eyes and mine.

THE CELEBRATION

The summer they were married they returned
to his parents' house, a place of broad days and broader darknesses,

sketched by grass-patched dirt roads and hay fields gone to seed.
From the newly-painted barn the father brought a box

of fireworks he'd collected and stored
in the son's absence, brightly-papered cones and rockets

leaning dusty from the cardboard. It was freshly night. Stars
were burning in and cooling in the blackness. The father

brought out strike-anywhere matches, a handful for the son, too,
one crimped in his mouth like a tailor's pin.

But the son was drawn to another light — his new bride
shimmering, shivering now in the towering dark, pulling across her

legs the sweatshirt she'd borrowed from him. The father
lit a small rocket, which shrieked into the air and was spent

with a brief flash and pop. Another. The son stood
beside his father, taking each firework from the box, freeing

the fuse and handing it to him. The rockets were damp
from their storage, coughing their small cargoes into the sky

unremarkably. A fountain tipped, spurted a fan of color
across the gravel drive. The son knew his wife was lonely,

surrounded by this darkness not her own, but he lingered
near his father, watched him by the globes of match light,

impatiently, fearfully waiting for the last small spark
to surge into the darkness — a quick, futile flash

before the black monument of sky.

Spring: I Imagine Your Burial

As the last of the crocuses
    open into the dawn,

the town's gravedigger
    cuts in cold sod

an outline for the bed they'll lay you in.
    His shovel handle's lovely,

dark and smooth, burnished by sweat,
    by his hard hands,

by the songs he sings
    while digging. He turns the brown grass back

and smells the still-cold earth
    and it is new to him, as it is every time

new to him: at every grave
    he smells the earth

for the first time.
    He savors the rising in his chest

it brings: something almost
    love, but more

familiar. His little song's
    for spring, for the dirt pulled back, and still

for you, more patient now than ever.
    Across the road,

a low stone fence
    contains a field of stones. In the shadow

of your stone, he opens up the ground
    the way a parent

might peel back sheets
    to settle in a weary child.

WE SHALL NOT ALL SLEEP

Behold, I shew you a mystery; we shall not all sleep,
but we shall all be changed. — I Corinthians 15:51

After the smell of lilies filled the tiny country church;
after we drove down valleys and across mountains
through winter rain and fog and dissipating

snow; after the funeral director
took our coats and intoned in a low voice
his professional compassion, a kind

of snow itself; after the unexpected shock
of first seeing the coffin; after the townsfolk
and childhood friends moved through, offering

their condolences, and after we shifted from one foot to the other
beneath the burden of their sympathy;
after the remembrances, after the sons, the daughter,

their sons and daughters, after the old
farmhand, the surviving sister, and the neighbor who one winter
took all his meals beside her fire remembered her

kindness and good humor as we
suffered our own memories of her kindness and good humor;
after the preacher mounted his podium

and said *For God so loved the world* and
If Christ be not raised;
after we took or did not take

our consolations in the miracle of the Resurrection, and after
the fugitive sun shone through the stained-glass shock of wheat
just so, we gathered in the church basement

around long tables and ate.
The United Methodist Women fed us ham and potato salad,
Jell-O with fruit suspended inside.

We remembered to each other
that she, the absent one, had been one of these women,
had served food and spoken kindly

to the families of old farmers who had died in their hard beds
or in the dust of the fields, and had received
this kindness, too, upon the death of one husband

and then another, as outside
the rain began again.
One of the United Methodist Women cried

remembering her own dead husband, and was consoled.
Upstairs, in the empty sanctuary, the coffin
and its contents removed, I sat alone

in a middle pew. Through the floor
came voices
rising and falling together.

THREE

LEAVINGS

1

Kansas is as good a place to leave as any,
but any leaving feels like loss.
I lost Kansas in a compact car
in the middle of America.
Of course there was a girl there.
There is always a girl.
We walked a railroad track at night
to a clearing where an old stove rusted
by a stream. Our hands
touched lightly, like two trout,
while our eyes adjusted to the dark.
No stars.

2

Outside Booneville, Missouri,
I slept three hours in my car
and woke before dawn.
I woke
to shattered headlights,
their tiny bodies cracked in the night
by some peculiar atmosphere,
some unseen hand. This light
was left: one high beam. I
drove east, my one good eye
pitched to the horizon, digging
by starlight, myself a star
throwing light across the universe
until the dark
dissolved in the accumulating sky,
and the sunrise glowed and gathered
between the tall buildings of St. Louis.

3

Across the deeply furrowed
bedrock of Kentucky, I forgot
my name. Old, arthritic men
led thoroughbreds from stables, fed them oats
by hand, whispered in their ears. These men,
who spat into the Ohio
where Clay
had thrown his medals.
These men,
who smelled of bourbon
and molasses. Their horses,
sleek and regal, flesh quivering,
aching to run.

4

West Virginia
is full of empty mines. I slept near one.
I slept a miner's sleep that night,
though all the miners are in Alloy
drinking coffee at the Dinerette,
clapping each other on the back
in greeting, smoking cigarettes
and slowly going blind.
All night, a long fern
brushed the fabric of my tent.
A deer crept by
and bowed her head.
I dreamed I was a miner,
hands coal-darkened on the pick,
digging in what little light there was.

5

By Fulton, you begin to feel the lake.
The air grows ripe with water.
The locks on the Oswego stand
unused, and fill with carp.
This land is full of graves.
At Fort Ontario, twelve slanted stones
shade twelve green mounds shot through with roots
of giant maple trees.
The lake sits heavy in its casket,
and the ground's body heaves.

6

I slept beside the sea.
Outside my tent,
clams gurgled in the muck
in the low tide at dawn.
And the clamdiggers came
with forks and buckets and waded
in the muck to the tops of their boots.
I woke a little.
Dew-soaked light
seeped into the corners of my dream.
A bird was singing: *see, see, see.*
The ocean edged closer to the land,
filling in the bootprints
one by one.

DOWSING

beneath thirsty grass

                                  beneath my dumb feet

beneath humus soil stone bone

                                        something flows in a life

that asks nothing of me

                                these sticks

slack in my grip

                          bow and nod

one to the other

                        graze lightly together

in spite of me

                    I listen carefully and hear nothing

wait to be pulled

                        and am not pulled

wait to be touched

                            but these sticks

in my hand — water

however silent

however deep

has something

to say to them

and they listen

ON WATER

for R and A

Return yourselves
          to the sea.
     Return to its

brine-smell, its vagrant
          tidal edge,
     to the spangles

of light that fire
          its surface.
     Close your eyes

along the shoreline
          and listen to it
     break

against the sand
          without breaking.
     Leave the open

razor clam
          half-buried in the muck,
     the shore-washed jellies

drying on the sand.
          Build a driftwood fire
     and let the tide

erase it. Return
          to the sea,
     where all water

begins and ends,
                   where,
          in sunlight,

water vapor
                   rises
          into the bellies

of clouds
                   where it gathers —
          on ashes, on bits of dust —

before it falls
                   as rain again
          over the sea,

and over the land beside the sea,
                   and over people
          standing in the open

or sheltered in houses
                   eating or praying, alone
          or looking into

another's eyes.
                   Take as comfort
          the rain's

indifference:
                   its hands are cool,
          but not unkind.

Second Attempt at Elegy
for Anthony Piccione

Last night I climbed once more
the narrow ladder
of my poems.

I took my fine pen
and turned paper
into ash.

What were you
turned into?
What did you become,

after?

Once you said
that to write a poem
is to touch the unseen.

If I have touched the unseen,
it has not been in my poems,
in their labored breaths

and gesticulations.
Perhaps I touched it reaching
with gloved and gentle hand

for the bat trapped
in the flue, or when
the doe,

surprised in the field's raw stubble,
bowed her head to me
and did not run.

Perhaps to suffer kindness
is to touch the unseen.
Last night I listened

hard into the dark.
I was waiting
for a poem to you.

That listening
was my kindness.

There is much
that was unseen.

THE DARKNESS OF THE ROOM

I am hearing well tonight.
It is not always so.
I do not always hear so well,
but now, so late, with the rumbling
taxis and Novas sighing their
loud exhaust up and down the street,
and the lights from the halfway house
all out but the one TV
still flickering its blue into
the darkness of the room,
I hear myself say
the darkness of the room
although I'm quiet here,
and the sirens have begun again,
and I realize I prefer it
to *room's darkness* or even
room's dark because
the time it takes to say *the darkness*
of the room inside
your mind and hear yourself
is like the waiting that a man does
in the middle of the night,
his car idle by the sidewalk.
He is not waiting for anyone
or anything to happen.

WEST NILE

Tonight, in the suburbs, they are spraying
the disease.

They have found out who the enemy is.

Out all night, spraying,
every street, every lawn.

Children are finding dead birds in their backyards:

sparrows and crows, feathers disheveled,
eyes black and open.

Cats won't touch them, with the virus.

So tonight they're out spraying, and one driver is lonely and tired
and eating a sandwich as his truck crawls up Oak Street toward
Delphi, with the radio whispering static and the tires making sighing
noises on the pavement and

he finds he is not watching the road but
counting streetlights and stop signs and once in a while a cat

with a crushed head on the lip of a storm drain

distracts him from thoughts of his loneliness, his sandwich, the poison
that kills the mosquitoes,

that varnishes the lawns,

that settles on the tongues of the sleeping.

ABOVE GROUND

I had seen by that time two or three
Holes in the ground,
And you know what they were.
         — James Wright

Because of the way the river runs,
because the earth is empty
and the stones won't burn,
I am where my father never was: above
the mines, hands pink, nails scrubbed.

You can tell the tourists —
no West Virginian will look down
an empty hole. They've seen too many,
seen too many of them filled.

Families from Pittsburgh and Ohio
make wishes over tossed coins.
Their children lean against the railings shouting
into the hole's mouth, and then they listen
as the blackness eats their voices.

At night, when I sleep, and the sign
outside creaks like a cross-beam
just before the ceiling goes,
I dream this hole is filled with gold, with milk,
with my body, while the earth expires under
the weight of the dim-eyed miners
lurching slowly toward the ground.

Dairy Farm, January

It has been this cold for months.
Your hands are chapped to bleeding, and
the shadow of the silo creeps across the ground.

Your cattle are dying.
You phone the vet, change their feed,
pray, do what you can.

When one goes down
you stumble through the frozen shit to the stall
where she labors and snorts. She's the fourth one

down this week. You kick her
in the ribs, *Come on.* You try to care
about her. What you really want

is to climb up to the hay loft with a rope
and hang yourself among the rotting straw
and pigeon shit, or set fire to the house and settle
in the soft mud beneath the frozen pond,

but instead you kick her in the ribs again.
She shifts but can't stand up.
If this one dies, you say out loud,

I'm done. I won't do this anymore.
You make a bet with God that there is life beyond
this farm. You kick the cow again, hard, and

she struggles and gets up. She rolls her eyes,
chews her cud, and lurches from the stall.
You take her in and milk her.

THE DRIVER FROM THE RENDERING PLANT

The man who dragged the dead cow, frozen stiff,
across the shitty concrete floor with winch
and cable sits inside his truck and cries.
He's hiding from you what you'll never see —
when he comes back, he smiles, his crooked teeth
a yellowed mess. His eyes are red, you think,
from lack of sleep. He has a family in Hornell,
two hours' drive from here. He writes a check
for fifty-five, the going rate for cows.
(A stillborn calf brings only ten, because
he loads it in the truck by hand.) You take the check
and thank him, glad the cold keeps down the smell.
He wants to shake your hand. Instead, you wave.

Against Reading

I looked hard beyond the symbol to the dove
that labored on the lawn, its head bowed
as though it had lost something —
loose change, a button, a bottle cap —
among the browning grass.
It was easier somehow, from the window
at my desk, to place a meaning on
the strewn feathers and cracked neck:
my own lament at our latest war. So I went
outside to see him. He flapped wildly
at my approach but could not fly. By evening,
a stray cat would have him, would leave
a little blood, one half-plucked wing; until then,
he'd hang his head and wait.
From behind the shed, I took the broken
handle of a hoe, apologized, and struck him
once above the eyes.

THE ROOSTER

His frowning beak, his fleck-of-granite eye.
Against the rough pine planks he beats his wings,
and dirty feathers drift across the yard.
I feel that dark, blank eye on me. He struts
atop the coop as though he hears my heart
pounding in its fist-tight cage. I turn my back,
reluctant, and scan the ground for the morning's eggs.
A brown one rests beside the water trough.
Its perfect oval is a poem, one
I've tried to write, about the planet's orbit
and charts describing Earth's trajectory.
I cradle it; my palm repeats the shape.
Then I feel a quick, sharp thump on my anklebone,
and a perfect bloody flower blossoms there.

THE LAST MEAL OF FRANÇOIS MITTERAND

Cancer spreads like oil
through the gutters of his body.
Wracked with pain and dulled by drugs,
he sleeps between courses, wakes for oysters,
then pâté, then a fat capon baked in wine,
and last, a songbird, drowned in brandy, plucked
and eaten whole: the ortolan.
He pulls a towel atop his head to shield him
from the sight of God, then severs
the head and holds the tiny teardrop body
on his tongue. He leans back in his chair,
eyes closed, weak from the effort
of tasting. And then he chews.

The bird bursts between his teeth: bitter organs,
succulent meat, a tiny gout of Armagnac.
Barely conscious, he grinds the tiny ribcage down,
splits the heart with his incisors and wishes
he could sing. He drowns in taste,
it fills his lungs. He knows
he will be dead by morning.

THE CLAWFOOT TUB

The day after Ray's son died,
he came to help us gut the old
farmhouse. Chris had quit his job

two months before —
no one knew how bad things
had become.

We carried everything
outside: the davenport,
the iron stove, the battered

knives from the kitchen drawers, even
the clawfoot tub got dragged out
on the lawn. With hammer

and prybar and saw
we tore up linoleum,
smashed through plasterboard,

splintered cabinetry.
We broke the back
steps, shattered

the delicate woodwork
on the banister.
We were reckless

and artistic
in our destruction, fervent
in our diligence.

Ray had found Chris in his bathroom
dead and purpled, pants around his knees —
pancreatitis and a liver fat with drink.

One month, almost to the day,
my younger. In two days,
Ray would take the ashes to the hill

and spread them
in the corner of a field. And so
we pulled the ceilings down,

pried out the sink
and left it by the road.
When the day began to fail,

we went outside and watched
the last light linger in the sockets
where the windows had been.

A dog barked in the valley.
Ray's cigarette
smoldered in the early dark

like a great disaster
seen from far away.

Requiescat for Terri Schiavo

If I say
      they let you die
   I am saying I believe

in death as a force
        given into,
     not a breaking

from but a turning
        back to,
     the way falling

is a return,
        the way your body,
     when it sagged

toward death,
        was relinquished to it,
     was let down

into the ground
        and covered over.
     Gravity

is a short tether,
        and when you died
     you were like a boat

returned to the water,
        you were like water
     returned to the ground.

But what does gravity
        return? What rises? Your
    soul? Loaves

rise, born
        in a baker's hands.
    The bread

held high by the priest,
        broken
    above a cup

of wine,
        the bread that is
    the body

rises. The smoke
        from the oven.
    The sun. These human voices.

After rain, mist
        rises from the forest,
    meaning the rain is over.

For a Burial

If you have slipped your hand
　　inside the bright machinery of a deer,
　　　　and felt the veined heart spasm and subside;

if you have shot a woodchuck in a field
　　and plugged its burrow with the body;
　　　　if you have pressed a wounded pheasant's head

beneath your boot until
　　its wings stopped pounding, you know
　　　　what futile stuff a body's made of. If you

have seen the graveyards
　　where the dead are sealed
　　　　against decay, if you have seen mausoleums,

and corpses cased in glass,
　　you know that humans say *remains*
　　　　as a command —

and you know why.
　　For you have seen the maple trees
　　　　whose roots upturn the gravestones,

and you have seen the grass
　　grown lush beyond the slaughterhouse.
　　　　The body disappears,

soaks into the ground, and grows again.
　　The woodchuck always was the burrow
　　　　into which its body slides.

When I die, leave me where my body
     can embrace the body of the ground.
        Till me deep into the soil, and

plant your garden there.
     Your tomatoes will grow rich with me.
        Eat them quartered, with a little salt,

beside an open window.
     Let their juice speak on your tongue:
        it is my breath.

About the Author

Shane Seely is a Senior Lecturer in the English Department at Washington University in St. Louis, where he teaches composition and creative writing and acts as Assistant Director of the university's freshman writing program. A native of northern Pennsylvania, he was educated in Pennsylvania, Kansas, and New York. He earned an MFA in creative writing at Syracuse University. He lives in St. Louis with his wife and their dog.